God Cares About Sports

Your 30-Day Spiritual Training Manual

Daryl Jones

Copyright © 2016 Daryl Jones

All rights reserved. No part of this book may be reproduced, stored in a retrieval system, or transmitted in any form or by any means – electronic, mechanical, photocopying, recording, or otherwise – without the prior written permission of the publisher and the copyright owner. The only exception is brief quotations in printed reviews.

7710-T Cherry Park Dr, Ste 224
Houston, TX 77095
(713) 766-4271
www.WorldwidePublishingGroup.com

The views expressed in this book are those of the author and do not necessarily reflect those of the publisher.

Published in the United States of America.

Ebook: 978-3-9602-8635-6

Paperback: 978-0692707302

Hardcover: 978-1-60796-990-7

Table of Contents

Introduction 5

1 A Strong Foundation 7

2 You Are Not What You Do 9

3 No Fear Here.. 11

4 Attitude Adjustment 13

5 The Main Ingredient 15

6 Consistency 17

7 OPPOSITION: An Athlete's Greatest Promotor 19

8 Be A Team Player 21

9 Work Hard 25

10 FAITH: Believing Is Seeing 27

11 Glorify God In All You DO 29

12 Cast Your Care On Him 31

13 EXCELLENCE: Always Give Your Best.................. 33

14 LEARNING: Your Pathway To Growing 35

15 LEADERSHIP: It's All About Influence 37

16 Making Each Other Better 39

17 Success Is Not A Destination; It's A Journey 41

18 Money Is An Excellent Tool, But A Terrible Master 45

19 Self-Control 47

20 Humility 49

21 CHARACTER: Will The Real You Please Stand Up? 51

22 Sowing=Reaping 53

23 Success Is Intentional 57

24 You Only Have One Body 59

25 Birds Of A Feather Flock Together 61

26 Stay Focused. Pay Attention. 63

27 We Love God Because He First Loved Us 65

28 Meditation 67

29 Visualization, The Next Step To Goal Achievement 69

30 Sticks And Stones May Break Your Bones And Words WILL Hurt You 71

Prayer for Salvation 73

15 Positive Affirmations For Athletes 75

The Author 77

Introduction

Did you know that you have greatness inside you right now that the entire world is waiting to see? God has given you gifts, talents and abilities to benefit not only yourself but others as well. He finds great pleasure in the success of His children. Any success you desire in your life as an athlete starts inside of you, in your thinking.

A wise man once said, "Godly words produce godly thinking, godly thinking produces godly emotions, godly emotions produce godly decisions, godly decisions produce godly actions, godly actions produce godly habits, godly habits produce godly character, and godly character produces godly destinations in your life." Believe it or not, every success or failure that happens to you as an athlete starts with the words to which you are exposed.

If you can change your thinking, you can change your life and ultimately your destination. I have been around many great athletes who seemed to do everything right when it came to hard work and physical training, only to see them crumble under pressure while never really reaching their true potential. Is it possible to be the hardest worker on your team, follow the lessons that the world's greatest coaches have taught you, and still never reach your full potential?

I have good news. You can indeed reach your full potential. Inside this book, you will find the necessary tools to help unlock the hidden mystery of true fulfillment. Maybe you have been trying to prepare a recipe for success that hasn't tasted quite right. A magnificent entrée takes time, effort, and a mixture of unique ingredients. These special ingredients embody any great athlete. This 30-day training manual gives you the missing ingredients for success.

So rejoice, because today is the start of your deliverance from the old negative thinking that has kept you bound in the chains of mediocrity. As you tackle each day, let God exchange your thoughts for His thoughts and enjoy the freedom of this new life of success that God always intended.

Daryl Jones

1
A Strong Foundation

"I can do all things through Christ who strengthen me and empowers me." Philippians 4:13, AMP

The success of any athlete, regardless of the sport that he plays, depends on the strength and the supporting the foundation of their bodies. For example, in baseball, your legs are the foundation or support system that determines what your other body parts will do next.

The baseball swing starts with the legs. If you have a strong foundation with your legs, and allow them to do most of the work in your swing, you learn that your upper body (stomach, shoulders, hands and head) remains stable and fluid. As a result, you instantly become a more powerful hitter because your legs, which are your foundation, are your true source of power.

If you try to supply all of your power using your upper body while neglecting the importance of your legs, you will always find yourself fighting to hit for power but never really reaching your full power potential.

Likewise, in our everyday lives, we face similar battles. We often try to build and better ourselves on our own, without having a strong foundation of God's Word. We aim for optimal performance each day, striving to achieve success, without realizing that if we wish to see certain fruit, we must start with the root.

Philippians 4:13 clearly conveys the thought that we are empowered to do *all* things through Christ. God wants our lives to display His power. When Christ is our foundation, the power we realize in life becomes exponential.

You don't have to fight alone. Allow Christ to be your power source and watch how He eases your burden. Remember: the stronger your foundation, the more powerful you are.

Prayer for Today:

Heavenly Father, thank you for wanting to be part of my life. Thank You for being my support in everything that I do. Help me stay strong and grounded in Your Word so that I can display my full power potential today. In Jesus' Name, Amen.

2
You Are Not What You Do

The Lord doesn't see things the way you see them. People judge by outward appearance, but the Lord looks at the heart. 1 Samuel 16:7, NLT

Players often place their value solely on their previous game, whether good or bad. If you had a three-hit game, you likely walk away from that game with a smile on your face. On the other hand, if you had a no hits game or a poor performance, you'll most likely have the opposite reaction because the results were different. Sports, in general, are for the most part results-driven.

Players want certain results, coaches want certain results, and even fans want certain results. One of the most significant conflicts a ballplayer can have is an inability to separate who he is as a ballplayer (his identity), and his results (his performance). Confusing who we are with what we do can create inner conflict. One who views his performance on the field as determining his value as a player is in for one heck of a roller coaster ride.

A good game inspires confidence, but a poor game can lead to insecurity and disappointment. To be a consistent ballplayer, you must have consistent confidence. Real confidence is believing in your ability regardless of the game's outcome. The more confidence you have in the athlete God made you, the more enhanced your performances will be. People will lose confidence in you, and at times you may lose confidence in you, but God never will.

God sees you the same no matter what other people say or think. According to this Scripture, God doesn't change His mind about you based on your performance on the field. He sees your greatness and potential because He created you with them. You are His beloved child. He sees the good in you no matter what. Don't allow your outward performance to determine your value. To God you are valuable because of who you are, not because of what you do.

Prayer for Today:

Heavenly Father, thank You for seeing the best in me at all times. Thank You for helping me develop confidence in my true identity as a child of God. Help me to put more trust in what You say about me, than what others think about me. In Jesus' Name, Amen.

3
No Fear Here

For God did not give us a spirit of timidity (cringing and craving and fawning fear) *but He has given us a spirit of power and of love and a calm and well-balanced mind with discipline and self-control.* 2 Timothy 1:7, AMP

Have you ever walked up to the plate thinking, "Uh-oh, I hope I don't strike out?" Or have you been in the field hoping the baseball wouldn't be hit to you? How about, "Man, I hope this guy doesn't crush this ball I'm about to throw?" What do all three of these statements have in common? Fear. Believe it or not, this is an ongoing battle for many ballplayers.

Nearly all of us battle with fear at times. Sometimes we approach a situation so worried that something bad will happen that we completely lose focus on the good that can happen. Each of us, at some point, fails to meet our expectations with the wrong mindset.

Stepping up to the plate trying *not* to strike out will usually lead us to strike out. Trying *not* to make an error in the field or trying *not* to walk a hitter often leads to exactly that. When you approach the game with fear, you eliminate any chance of having a positive outcome.

As you can see from this Scripture, God does not give us a spirit of fear; nor does He intend for us to live in fear. He does not enjoy seeing His children fearful. He knows that fear limits our opportunity for greatness.

I challenge you today, instead of approaching situations trying not to mess up, approach them with confidence, expecting the best result.

Prayer for Today:

Heavenly Father, thank you that you have not given me a spirit of fear, I thank you for helping me approach today with boldness and confidence. I expect a good outcome. In Jesus' Name, Amen.

4
Attitude Adjustment

Have this same attitude and purpose and [humble] *mind be in you which was in Christ Jesus* [Let Him be your example humility]. Philippians 2:5, AMP

The attitude you bring to the ballpark each day can contribute to the success of your team. Having a positive and energetic attitude around your teammates can make the difference in how your team plays that day. It is easy to think about how badly yesterday's game was, or how mad your parents or a friend made you before you left the house.

Like it or not, your attitude can affect the people around you in a good way, or it can affect them in a bad way. The more self-centered we are, the less team-minded we will be. When we bring a negative attitude to the field, our teammates can sense it. It will have one of two results: to make someone else's attitude negative or make someone else simply move away from you.

Take Jesus Christ, for example. He had every reason to be mad; people ridiculed Him and even tried to kill him. All He ever did was help people better their lives, yet look how He was treated.

Regardless, He maintained a great attitude and reconciled billions of people to God. He focused on others more than himself. He gave others the advantage, rather than take advantage. Make yourself a better player today by using your positive attitude to brighten up someone else's day.

Prayer for Today:

Heavenly Father, thank You for allowing me to play this awesome game of baseball. Thank You for strengthening and encouraging me to be a positive influence on my teammates. Remind me of all the good things I have for which to be thankful. In Jesus' Name, Amen.

5
The Main Ingredient

Therefore, prepare your minds for action, keep sober in spirit, fix your hope on the grace to be brought to you at the revelation of Jesus Christ. 1 Peter 1:13, NASB

You would be surprised at how many ballplayers spend their whole lives eating, sleeping, and waking up to sports. They spend several hours a day working on their physical abilities to help them perform better on the field but never reach their full potential because they never come to the point of understanding what I am about to share with you.

Contrary to popular belief, success does not come from your skill set and hard work. Yes, having good skills and hard work can help you achieve a certain level of success, but without one main ingredient, your performance cannot reach its maximum capacity. What is this missing ingredient? Your mindset.

Training your mind is more important in the long run than training your body because everything starts with your mind. Your body is the instrument that carries out what's in your mind. Your mind is the cockpit, and your body is the plane. Whatever happens in the cockpit determines what happens with the plane. Your plane can be the most beautiful plane, with the best fuel in it, but if you have someone in the cockpit who is not trained to fly the plan, it will eventually crash.

Likewise, without training our minds to be positive we are lessening our ability to perform well consistently, especially under pressure. According to this Scripture, God says that we are to prepare our minds. Just like we train our bodies through practice, we must train our mind through practice.

Reading a Scripture from the Bible or listening to a sermon or closing your eyes and picturing yourself doing something positive are all examples of training your mind. Start training your mind today through God's Word and you will begin to display your full potential, by filling your mind with godly thoughts of victory rather than defeat.

Prayer for Today:

Heavenly Father, thank You for giving me all the resources I need to be a complete player. Thank You for helping me control my mind so that I can perform well under pressure. In Jesus' Name, Amen.

6
Consistency

Jesus Christ is the same yesterday, today, and forever.
Hebrews 13:8, NLT

Has any coach or player ever told you that, "Practice makes perfect, or perfect practice makes perfect?" Although it is a seemingly timeless and catchy phrase, it's only half true. Practicing something over and over again will produce a result, but practice alone does not guarantee perfection. No matter your talent level, you will most likely never get to the point when you stop and say, "I'm done. I've reached perfection."

No matter how well you perform, that driving voice in your head and heart will continue to encourage you to strive for more. The fact that you continue to practice means that you have not reached perfection, which is a good because the moment you as a ballplayer stop learning, you stop improving. On the other hand, I have come to understand that, "Practice makes consistent."

The more you practice the right way, the more consistent you will become. Consistency simply means always to act or behave in the same way. Talent and athleticism don't necessarily produce results. Consistency produces results. The only difference between an average player and a great player is the great player can produce more often than the average player.

Hall of Fame players are not great because they've had one good season. Greatness involves the ability to duplicate quality performances season after season. What makes Jesus Christ so awesome is that when it comes to you and me, His love and mercy for us is consistent regardless of what we do. He never changes His good feelings or His great plan for you.

Jesus is the perfect example of someone who is consistent. He wants us to be consistent in all we do so we can see the wonderful results from being the same yesterday, today, and forever.

Prayer for Today:

Father, thank you for being the perfect example of what real consistency is. Thank You for always loving me regardless of my past mistakes. Help me to be consistent in my practice time so that I can be the best version of me that You created me to be. In Jesus' Name, Amen.

7
OPPOSITION: An Athlete's Greatest Promotor

In all these things we are more than conquerors, and gain a surpassing victory through Him who loved us. Romans 8:37, AMP

Facing opposition is part of every ballplayer's job. Whether facing another team whose goal is to defeat you, or playing a game in bad weather, opportunities abound to meet with opposition. People often perceive opposition as a negative. We dislike opposition, especially when it is inconvenient or not in line with our plans. Answer this question: Would it be possible to play a game without an opponent? How would you be able to enjoy a great season without great opponents?

Would you be able to get stronger in the gym without having to lift that heavy weight that is trying to push or pull your muscles in the opposite direction? Without the opposition from the weights, our muscles would never be able to grow and get stronger. Opposition makes us better than we were before we encountered it. It reveals our weaknesses, but also allows us to demonstrate our strengths. It shows us the areas where we still need to grow. It forces us to get creative and step out of our comfort zone which is needed to take us to the next level.

Imagine if you always saw opposition as an opportunity for improvement, rather than something to avoid. It is possible. However, it begins when you see yourself as an *overcomer.* The Bible says that we are more than conquerors through the love of Christ. A conqueror is someone who dominates, instead of being dominated. Seeing yourself as a conqueror allows you to face your trial with boldness rather than fear.

No matter what you face today, know and believe that you are a more than a conqueror and nothing can stop you or stand in your way.

Prayer for Today:

Father, thank You for making me an overcomer. I know that with Your help nothing can stop me. Help me to see my trials as an opportunity to grow rather than a threat. Thank You for encouraging and empowering me with Your love. In Jesus' Name, Amen.

8
Be A Team Player

Two are better than one because they have a more satisfying return for their labor; for if either of them falls, the one will lift up his companion. But woe to him who is alone when he falls and does not have another to lift him up. Ecclesiastes 4:9-12, AMP

There is never any great success achieved alone. Every success requires a team. Whether you compete on a two-man team or a sixty-man team, your success requires the help of someone else, and their success requires your help as well. One of the best ways to build a great organization or a great team is to build up the people *in* the organization or team. Any leader who neglects to encourage his followers will eventually fail.

The best team players are the ones who are willing to sacrifice their immediate needs and meet the needs of others. It may mean taking a moment to stop and praise your teammate for doing a drill the right way, or for making a nice play. The best teammates give more than they take away. A good teammate enjoys sharing his successes with his teammates. Good teammates understand that their actions can help or hinder their team's progress. They are willing to stand for what is right and what they believe without compromise.

That type of strength and character usually attracts and strengthens others around them. As you can see in Ecclesiastes, God specifically makes it clear that the more team players you have to back you up the better off you will be.

During His ministry on earth, Jesus surrounded himself with twelve disciples. The twelve disciples were a small group of people who knew Jesus on a more intimate level than anyone else. Jesus shared not only His trials but also His triumphs with His disciples, which is important because in sports we often face situations when we may fail to come through for the team, but we have someone else step up and succeed in our place.

Regardless of who succeeds, the whole team benefits from one person having success. Today, because one man, Jesus, sacrificed His life for us, we all now have the ability to share in all the wonderful blessings that God has offered to us. Jesus is the ultimate example of being a team player.

Prayer for Today:

Father, thank You for the wonderful sacrifice of Your Son Jesus, because of His sacrifice I am now able to enjoy a wonderful relationship with You and celebrate with others around me. Teach me to be a team player just like Jesus was. In Jesus' Name, Amen.

9
Work Hard

Lazy people want much but get little, but those who work hard will prosper. Proverbs 13:4, NLT

Today we live in a fast-paced, multi-tasked, high-tech society. With so much happening, it is often hard to focus and completely concentrate on one single task. It is very difficult to work hard on anything if your attention is always on multiple tasks at one time. If you fail to have a good work ethic, success will be difficult to sustain. Working hard does not guarantee success because of so many factors that may be involved in a situation, but working hard is an extremely important characteristic to have if you want real success.

In 1 Corinthians 15:10, TLB, the Apostle Paul says, *"But whatever I am now it is all because God poured out such kindness and grace up me, and not without results: for I have worked harder than all the other apostles, yet actually I wasn't doing it, but God working in me, to bless me."*

Paul clearly admitted that he worked harder than any other preacher of his time, but the awesome part is that he knew and understood that he was not the reason he worked so hard. He understood that it was God's power on the inside of him that had strengthened and built him up to be able to work so hard. His relationship with God the Father empowered him to be the best at whatever he did.

Sports is no different than your relationship with God. The amount of time and effort you put into it directly relates to the success you experience. You cannot put in only 25% of your effort and expect 100% back in return. Paul put his entire life into what he was called to do, which was to preach the Gospel of Jesus Christ. By doing that, Paul allowed God to fill him fully and entirely with His energy and power.

God wants you to get good results in your life too. He wants to energize you to be the best on and off the field. By spending time with Him and developing your relationship with Him, you can be empowered to enjoy all of the success God desires for you.

Prayer for Today:

Father, I thank You for caring about every area of my life. I know that you want me to succeed not only on the field but off the field as well. Thank You for empowering me to work hard in everything I do. In Jesus' Name, Amen.

10
FAITH: Believing Is Seeing

But when you ask him, be sure that you really expect him to tell you, for a doubtful mind will be as unsettled as a wave of the sea that is driven and tossed by the wind.
James 1:6, TLB

Have you ever stepped into your game and believed that a bad result was about to happen? Then all of a sudden, the negative image that was stuck in your head became a reality? Every athlete has experienced this one time or another. The truth is that in that very moment you still had faith. You had faith in a lie. You see, faith is to believe something that hasn't happened yet. As an athlete, you will always have two choices to make. You can believe what God says about you, or you can believe what other people say about you.

1 Timothy 4:4 says, *"Everything God made is good."* If everything God made is good, then we should always rejoice because God created us. We should look ourselves in the mirror and remind ourselves of how good we are. That is the truth about us. People around you may look at you and talk about how bad you are as a player because they judge you based on your outward appearance and performance.

On the other hand, God's judgment is based on your *inward* appearance. When you have faith in Jesus Christ, God sees you the same way He sees Jesus, beautifully and wonderfully made. To believe anything else other than that would be to believe a lie. As you get ready for today, remind yourself about how awesome, gifted, and talented you are, and be the great player God is making you.

Prayer for Today:

Father, thank You for seeing me the same way that You see Jesus, beautifully and wonderfully made. Thank You for all of the gifts and talents that You have given me. In Jesus' Name, Amen.

11
Glorify God In All You DO

Don't hide your light! Let it shine for all; let your good deeds glow for all to see, so that they will praise your heavenly Father. Matthew 5:16, NIV

Have you ever wondered why coaches drool over having good players on their teams? Not to say that coaches don't enjoy working with lesser skilled players at times, but every coach loves to see his players perform at their very best. Why? When a team performs well on a consistent basis, it makes the coach or the person in control look good. The players on the team are individual representatives of the coach's program or system.

The coach's job is not to do everything for you as a player, but to equip, build, and train you to be the best possible player that you can be. A good coach wants your best skills and talents show out in a ball game. They understand that the better you play, the better the team looks, and the better he looks like a coach. On the other hand, when a team is not performing well, who gets the blame? The coach.

God is the ultimate coach. He has given you great talents and abilities to show off to the world. He doesn't want you to be afraid of being great because

He put greatness in you. When you are fearless and dare to give your best, God will make others notice it. The reason God wants others to see all of the good He put in you is because when you succeed, you make Him look good just like your coach. When others see how good you are, they are going to want to find out what it is that makes you so great.

Those are the greatest times to give God the glory, and tell about how good God is. Players tend to seek out the coach who has built and trained many successful athletes. It gives God great pleasure to make us successful athletes. I challenge you today to embrace the thought that God's wants to use your athletic abilities to bring others closer to him. Don't hold back, let your light shine today.

Prayer for Today:

Father, thank You for making me your representative. Cause me to let the gifts and abilities You put in me to bring You glory and magnify Your great name. In Jesus Name, Amen.

12
Cast Your Care On Him

Cast your cares on the Lord and he will sustain you; he will never let the righteous be shaken. Psalm 55:22, ESV

A very popular football star once said, "God doesn't care about football." Sadly many athletes have that same mindset. It is easy for athletes to separate God from everyday life which includes sports. The problem with that mindset is that many athletes allow sports to affect other areas of their lives like relationships, school, or family.

If sports can have a major impact on how you deal with others in your everyday life, then God certainly wants to be part of it. He wants to be involved in whatever you are involved in, even the small details that others ignore.

Have you ever had a great game and been so happy that you just had to talk about it to everyone over and over? On the other hand have you had a bad game and just sat there with built up anger waiting to let it out? You see, those are the times that God wants you to talk to Him as if He were your best friend. He wants to celebrate and comfort you regardless of your circumstances. It is so much easier to carry something heavy when you have His help.

He wants to take the weight off your shoulders so you can display your true talent. When you are upset, feel free to dump the entire load on Him and continue to develop as a player as you develop your relationship with your best friend, God.

Prayer for Today:

Father, thank You that I am never alone. Thank You for always being there to listen to me when I need someone to talk to. Thank You for carrying the load for me so that I don't have to be weighed down by my past mistakes. In Jesus' Name, Amen.

13
EXCELLENCE: Always Give Your Best

Then this Daniel became distinguished above all the other presidents and satraps, because an excellent spirit was in him. And the king planned to set over the whole kingdom.
Daniel 6:3, NASB

What type or quality of work do people get when they get you? Is your work excellent or average? In the sports world, people don't pay money to see average. They want to see the best of the best.

Excellence is a talent or quality which is unusually good and so surpasses ordinary standards. As you can see from this Scripture, Daniel stood out from among all his peers so much that the king decided to put Daniel in charge of the entire kingdom. Every athlete wants to be on top, but not every athlete will commit to excellence in the growth process. Daniel's success did not start from the outside; his success started from what he possessed on the inside, an excellent spirit.

Having an excellent spirit means that Daniel had already determined ahead of time to do things to the best of his ability, regardless of the circumstances.

While practicing a certain drill, it can be very easy and tempting just to go through the motions to finish the drill. Excellence means that every repetition is your best. If you don't determine ahead of time to give 100%, then you will likely not give your all while doing a drill designed for your benefit.

The commitment to give your best in practice when it doesn't matter statistically; shows what is really in your heart. If you give your best when it doesn't count, then you can be trusted to give your best when it does matter. Daniel gave his best to God, even when faced with the possibility of death when he was thrown into the lion's den for his disobedience to the king's command. In spite of his mistreatment, he stayed the same person even through hard times.

The result, Daniel was rewarded by the king and set over the entire kingdom. If you commit to excellence in the face of adversity, whether it's with your coach, your teammates or even the weather, and remain faithful to giving your best all of the time; you will enjoy success at the top. Great quality can't stay unnoticed for too long. God made you stand out.

Prayer for Today:

Father, thank You for giving me a spirit of excellence. I thank You that the same excellent spirit that was in Daniel is also mine. Thank You for motivating me to give my best all of the time no matter what is going on around me. In Jesus' Name, Amen.

14
LEARNING: Your Pathway To Growing

A wise man will hear and increase in learning, and a man of understanding will acquire wise counsel. Proverbs 1:5, NASB

Did you know that you as a player give your coaches a purpose in life? Without a player to teach and pass down wisdom to, a coach is insignificant. Likewise, without a coach a player is limited in his growth and purpose as well. Like success, growth in any area of your life must be done on purpose.

Growth is a continuous process. Some of the most successful athletes you see today took the time to gain as much knowledge as they could from someone who had already accomplished or been successful in sports. Anytime you decide not to learn; you choose to stunt your growth. According to Proverbs 1:5, a wise man is someone who continues to grow.

Your spiritual life works the same way. Jesus is the best coach who has ever walked this earth. He wants to pour out all of His wisdom and knowledge into your life so that you may continue to grow into the best version of you. Your needs as a person and an athlete give Jesus His purpose as our Lord and Savior.

His purpose is to help us in whatever situation we face. I encourage you to take the time to sit down and allow Jesus through His Word to teach you how to reign as a king in this present life. (Romans 5:17, AMP; Revelation 1:6, KJV)

Prayer for Today:

Father, thank You for committing Your life to helping me grow as a person and an athlete. I thank You for passing down to me Your wisdom and knowledge to give me an advantage in my life. In Jesus' Name, Amen.

15
LEADERSHIP: It's All About Influence

Do nothing from selfishness or empty conceit, but with humility of mind regard one another as more important than yourselves. Philippians 2:3, HCSB

Ask yourself one question. Would you want to be coached by *you*? Would you want to be *your* teammate? This question allows you to evaluate as to whether or not you are leading effectively. You don't have to be the head coach to be a leader.

Leadership is all about influence. To the extent that you can influence your peers or teammates for the better, will be the ability you will be able to gain followers and lead effectively. In sports, everyone on your team has some form of influence, but not everyone can obtain followers.

The best player on the team is not necessarily the best leader. You don't gain followers because you claim the top spot on the mountain. You gain followers because you get off of that mountain and go where the people are. You engage with them in their world that you might understand them better. According to Philippians 2:3, good leaders are those who put the needs of others ahead of their own and make others feel important.

It's impossible to be a great leader and be consumed and focused only on yourself. Jesus showed us the best way to lead effectively. If anyone had reason to boast and think more highly of Himself than anyone else, it was because He was God Himself, the Creator of all. Instead, Jesus made it clear that His purpose was not for people to serve Him, but for Him to serve others. You will be surprised to see how much better your overall performance in your game will be when you determine to make others better.

Teams look for great leaders who make them better, who will build up *all the members* of that team. Today decide to serve someone and allow them to see the love of Christ shine through you because that is what real leadership is all about.

Prayer for Today:

Father, thank You for teaching me how to be a great leader just like Jesus. Help me to defeat selfishness by putting the needs of my teammates and others first. Mold me into the effective leader that You called me to be. In Jesus' Name, Amen.

16
Making Each Other Better

Iron sharpens iron, and one man sharpens another.
Proverbs 27:17, ESV

Did you know that you were created to be in relationships with other people? God in His creative wisdom decided to connect us with unseen forces. These forces help us have either a good or a bad connection with people. It is your choice how you connect with people.

Have you ever heard someone continuously complain and say every imaginable negative statement? Did you notice how quickly your attitude may have changed when that happened? Either you joined them and began to speak negatively yourself, or you became annoyed because of the negativity brought your way.

Either way, that person's negative vibe or energy had the ability to influence and change your attitude for better or worse. It is important to understand this invisible power or force you possess on the inside of you.

The best leaders have learned to control this energy and use it in a positive way to make good connections and build others up. It is extremely important in sports to intentionally bring positive energy to your teammates and friends. You will find that more positive responses come back to you. The result is you both benefit.

Jesus Christ mastered this attitude. Jesus was one of the coolest guys to hang around because He dedicated His life to making others better. Anytime you are a blessing to someone; the blessing comes right back at you. That is the reason Jesus had so much joy regardless of what anyone else did or said to Him. He was simply too built up with the joy He had given to others.

Today, when you get around your team, make a decision to build others up around you, and you will soon receive energy and joy from what you gave to others.

Prayer for Today:

Father, thank You for the great energy that You put on the inside of me. Lead and guide me today to use this energy to build others up around me just like Jesus did. Thank You for making me a better leader and follower of Christ. In Jesus' Name, Amen.

17
Success Is Not A Destination; It's A Journey

You shall walk in all the way that the Lord your God has commanded you, that you may live, and that it may go well with you, and that you may live long in the land that you shall possess. Deuteronomy 5:33, ESV

In today's technological society we are exposed to very rapid and high paced living. The advances the world has made in this area has benefitted the economy in a great way. It has made it a lot easier and faster to do many things. The downside of that is a mindset that develops into what I call the *"I want it now"* mindset.

Exposure to an environment that makes things happen quickly can cause you to expect everything to happen fast. The world is constantly pumping wrong ideas about what success looks like, having shown luxurious lifestyles of famous athletes, expensive houses, and cars. There is nothing wrong with having fame, or enjoying a luxurious lifestyle, but none of that stuff makes you successful.

Success is not a certain point in life where you look at all the money and awards you have and say,

"I'm successful." Real success is fulfilling God's plan for your life. Reaching and staying in your God-given purpose is a lifetime process. Success is not a destination, but rather a journey. Think about the sport you play right now. You may have goals that you would like to reach, but the fact that you get out there and practice every day is proof that success is a journey.

If success were a destination, then after you had a good season or got an award you would have said, "Ok, I'm successful. I'm done." Instead, you prepared for the next season. No matter how well you do, there will always be a small voice inside of you that says, "Do even better next time."

The same is true of your relationship with God. Like any relationship, there is no time limit on how to build a successful relationship; it is a continuous process that improves over time if you stay the course.

Notice in Deuteronomy, God said *"walk."* He didn't say run. This process requires time to develop. Anything worth having requires time. During this process, you are guaranteed to make mistakes, but you should learn from them, and do it better next time. Remind yourself today that you don't have to rush, take your time and enjoy the process and allow God to prepare you for the success He has already reserved for you.

Prayer for Today:

Father, You know me more than anyone, You know the areas where I need to be more patient. Thank You for giving me Your supernatural peace that helps me stay calm and not rush ahead of Your plan for my life. Guide me to Your perfect will for my life. In Jesus' Name, Amen.

18
Money Is An Excellent Tool, But A Terrible Master

For the love of money is a root of all kinds of evil. Some people, eager for money, have wandered from the faith and pierced themselves with many griefs. 1 Timothy 6:10, NIV

Have you ever asked yourself why you want to play sports in the first place? Is it because you simply love the game, or is it because you see how your favorite athlete gets to be on television and have all of this money and be famous?

Many athletes are drawn to play sports in hopes of obtaining high professional salaries. Although there is nothing wrong with money, there is if it's your primary motive for being an athlete. A wrong attitude about money can lead you to do the craziest things that destroy your life.

If money is your sole purpose for being a professional athlete, then you are open yourself up to all kinds of trouble, because God made it very clear in Matthew 6:24 that, *"No one can serve two masters. Either you will hate the one and love the other, or you will be devoted to the one and despise the other. You cannot serve both God and money."*

Even with sports, God wants you to place Him first in your life. He wants to be your motivation for why you do what you do. He knows that money can easily be someone's master. It's hard to play for God when you are playing for money because your heart will not be focused primarily on God. When you keep God as your motivation for success in sports, it will always keep you from experiencing unnecessary pain, mentally and physically.

When God is 1st place, money and success will automatically come as a result, and you will not have to compromise your integrity and character to get it. Decide today to make God the motivation as to why you do what you do.

Prayer for Today:

Father, thank You for working on my heart to help me clarify my motives. Thank You for helping me keep you first in my life as my reason and motivation to play sports. In Jesus' Name, Amen.

19
Self-Control

A fool always loses his temper, but a wise man holds it back. Proverbs 29:11, NASB

If you have played sports long enough, you have most likely had plenty of opportunities to get upset or see others get upset during a ball game. Sports can be very emotional at times. It can bring out the best and worst in people. Quite often, players do not exercise self-control, which is a problem because for one to succeed athletically, he must be able to control himself.

A lack of self-control can lead you to do something that can hurt you or your team. Self-control is a characteristic which is extremely important to have for anyone in a leadership position, especially under pressure. The ability to feel negative emotions, but not act on them takes strength and the ability to see beyond your present circumstance.

Emotions were given to us by God to enjoy our lives on earth, but they were never meant to control us. Jesus displayed self-control on a daily basis during His ministry on earth. Many times he was faced with persecution and negative comments about who he was as a person. He did good to others, and in return was beat down emotionally time and time again.

If anyone had a reason just to go crazy on everyone, it was Jesus. He never sinned against anyone but was treated badly by so many. Jesus understood that He had to control His emotions to carry out His assignment for a greater purpose.

Had Jesus decided to take matters into His hands and try to defend Himself, He may have irrationally acted out of anger and given the people exactly what they needed to accuse Him of not being the Messiah. If that had occurred, you and I might not be here to talk about our wonderful salvation.

The next time your game takes a bad turn, remember that your team depends on you to hold your peace and stay focused on the greater goal.

Prayer for Today:

Father, thank You for giving me the ability to stand strong today under any difficult situation I may encounter. Lead me always to do what is best for myself and the entire team. In Jesus' Name, Amen.

20
Humility

A person's pride will bring about his down fall, but the humble in spirit will gain honor. Proverbs 29:23, ISV

One of the many temptations that you may face as an athlete is the thought that you are responsible for your success. Taking on that responsibility is dangerous because it crowns you as the source of your success rather than God.

When you see yourself as the source, you begin to depend on yourself for everything instead of God. Although, as an athlete you must work hard and sacrifice, God is the one responsible for giving you all of your talents and abilities. To think anything differently will lead you into the sin of pride. Pride is the opposite of humility. A prideful person lifts himself above others and tries to achieve success on his own rather than to trust God.

Pride is the sin that caused God to kick Satan, whose former name was Lucifer, out of heaven. God made him heaven's "music master." But when Satan saw how talented God had made him, he began to praise himself instead of the one who made him. Satan became so prideful that he wanted to take God's place and crown himself God. Well, that was obviously a big mistake. As an athlete, you will have plenty of opportunities to receive praise from others. The trap that can develop is when people begin to lift you up. At that point, it is easy to forget that it is God who gave you your abilities, and can result in you receiving the credit that God deserves.

When you stay grounded in the truth that God is your Source and give Him all the credit and glory for your success, He will lift you to higher places of influence to tell the world who is responsible for your great success.

Prayer for Today:

Father, thank You for giving me my talents and abilities. I know that You are the one who is responsible for all the good that happens to me. Help me to focus on You as my source and remind me constantly that I never have to try to achieve anything by myself because You are always with me. In Jesus' Name, Amen.

21
CHARACTER: Will The Real You Please Stand Up?

We rejoice in our sufferings, knowing that suffering produces endurance, and endurance produces character, and character produces hope, and hope does not put us to shame because God's love has been poured into our hearts through the Holy Spirit, who has been given to us.
Romans 5:3-5, ESV

Character can be defined as "doing what's right because it's right and doing it the right way." As an athlete, your true character is demonstrated in times of adversity. You will often face adversity. It is at that moment that your "true self" shows.

The easiest thing in the world to do is be happy-go-lucky and friendly when you've had a good game, and everything is going your way. The hardest thing to do is to be that same happy-go-lucky person when you just had the worst game of your life.

Sports is full of athletes who think they have great character because they cheer the team on when all is well in their world. That is not genuine. Show me the athlete who builds up his team regardless of the type of game they have had, and I will show you a man of good character.

Good character athletes remain consistent with their approach toward teammates. They have confidence and hope in something far greater than just having good stats. An athlete with good character is confident in his ability and doesn't need to show off to impress others. He rarely needs a coach or authority figure to stand behind him to see if he has done the drill with quality. Spiritually it is the same thing. A player with good character off the field has his values grounded in the Word of God and doesn't allow outside circumstances to change his beliefs or attitude.

Romans 5:3-5 indicates that a good character player rejoices no matter what, even in the face of suffering because he is grounded in the fact that God loves him, and nothing can stand in his way. As you go through today, determine to demonstrate good character regardless of the situation because you are a representative of Jesus Christ.

Prayer for Today:

Father, thank You for Your Word that gives me strength to remain faithful to my values as a child of God. Help me to demonstrate good character no matter what so that others may see my good works and give glory to You. In Jesus' Name, Amen.

22
Sowing=Reaping

As long as the earth endures, seed-time and harvest, cold and heat, summer and winter, day and night will never cease. Genesis 8:22, NIV

Have you ever been in an argument with your family member or friend and heard them say, "What goes around comes around?" What they were trying to get across to you is that whatever you do to someone else will be done back to you. More times than not, you will hear this statement used negatively, saying that something bad will happen to you.

In God's Kingdom, this is called the *Law of Seed-time and Harvest*. God created the earth so that the law of gravity works for and against everyone, the same is true of the law of seed-time and harvest. It will work for anyone who will get involved in it.

A farmer is a perfect example of someone who operates in this law. Whenever a farmer wants to harvest a crop, he must first plant seeds in the ground. A good farmer never expects to grow a huge crop without planting seeds in the ground, and then follow it up with day by day watering and sunlight. After continuously caring for the seeds, the farmer begins to see his precious seeds become plants that start to grow fruit and vegetables over time. It is a process.

One important concept to understand as well is that a farmer doesn't expect an apple tree to grow when he has planted corn. If he plants corn, then his expected crop will be corn because of the corn seed planted in the ground.

Likewise, seed-time and harvest work in the life of an athlete as well. In a sense, you are "a seed." The more you take care of your body, the more you practice, the more you learn and understand the techniques required for your sport, the more growth you will see in your sport. Anytime you take the time to practice or get better in your sport; it's like the farmer who daily waters his seed he put in the ground.

If the farmer decides to no longer water or give sunlight to the seeds, then the plant will not grow properly, and the harvest process will stop. If you, as an athlete, continue to water and give sunlight to your abilities by continuous practice, you can expect to grow into a beautiful, well-groomed athlete and have a harvest of great success.

Prayer for Today:

Father, thank You for helping me to plant good seeds in my life that will help me grow into the best person and athlete I can be. Thank You for helping me grow and have success in every area of my life. In Jesus' Name, Amen.

23
Success Is Intentional

He continued to seek God in the days of Zechariah, who had understanding through the vision of God; and as long as he sought the Lord, God prospered him. 2 Chronicles 26:5, NASB

What kind of success do you want in your life and sports? Do you want to make your high school team, to get a college scholarship, or to become a professional athlete? Whatever it is, you must understand that success in anything doesn't just happen. You accomplish it on purpose.

A strong relationship with God is vital if one is to experience success that can be passed to future generations. One must develop a good relationship with God on purpose. God will never make you come to Him. He will wait for you to come to Him because He wants you to choose Him on purpose.

When you start to build a successful relationship with God, every area of your life will benefit from it. Matthew 6:33 tells us to seek first the Kingdom of God and His righteousness, and He will provide everything else we need. Real success comes when you put God first in everything you do.

Just like sports, you can't go every day without practice and expect to get better or perform at your very best. The more you practice and take quality repetitions, the better you develop your skills.

Likewise, as you spend quality time with God, you can expect Him to make you the best version of you in whatever you do.

Prayer for Today:

Father, thank You that every day I have an opportunity to build my relationship with you, Thank You for causing me to be successful in everything I put my hands to. In Jesus' Name, Amen.

24
You Only Have One Body

A joyful heart is good medicine, but a crushed spirit dries up the bones. Proverbs 17:22, ESV

Have you ever seen anyone try to put water in the gas tank of a car and expect it to run properly? Better yet, have you seen anyone get upset with the car for not running when it has no gas in it? Probably not. A car needs the right amount of gas as well as the right type of gas to carry out its purpose.

Likewise, your body is just as important as the car you drive. As an athlete, your body is the vehicle that helps you perform on the field. Just like the car, your body needs the right food and enough water to perform at maximum strength.

As important as it is for you to put the right type of fuel in your body (physical man), it is even more important to understand how to properly feed your spirit (spiritual man). The best quality of food for your spirit is the Word of God (Bible). When you read the Bible, you feed and strengthen your spirit. To feed on God's Word is like taking medicine. It brings health and healing to your spirit, soul and body.

Many athletes focus on their physical training and fail to train spiritually. As a result, because they develop physical strength they can withstand physical pressure. But because they are spiritually undeveloped, they can't control their minds, wills or emotions. Everything starts on the inside of us. For example, anger doesn't start on the outside; it starts within. It's demonstrated on the outside.

Whatever you put on the inside will be seen on the outside of your life. Make a quality decision today to become a complete player by not only training physically but also training spiritually with the power of God's Word.

Prayer for Today:

Father, thank You for giving me Your Word to strengthen me spiritually as well as physically. Thank You for giving me all the tools that I will ever need to be the very best player that I can be. In Jesus' Name, Amen.

25
Birds Of A Feather Flock Together

Do not be deceived, bad company corrupts good morals. 1 Corinthians 15:33, NASB

One time I was standing on a chair and my friend was standing on the ground. The chair put me three to four feet taller than my friend. In an attempt to show my strength I bent down to wrap my arms around my friend to pick him up.

The result was a lot of stress on my back as I struggled to lift my friend maybe a foot off of the ground. When I finally let go, he grabbed my hand and gave a small tug and successfully pulled me off of the chair with ease. My friend was not nearly as strong as I was. So how did he manage to pull me down so easily?

In this, I learned a valuable life lesson. *It's much easier to pull someone down from a higher level than it is to lift one from a lower level.* Many times as an athlete we find ourselves as the spotlight of attention. As you rise to higher levels of competition, the praise and attention grow. You become a target for other people to want to be around. Since you are a child of God,

Satan constantly looks for different ways to knock you down. Many times it comes through the relationships closest to us.

The only true test to know whether you have surrounded yourself with the right type of friends is to know exactly where it is that you want to go yourself. Make no mistake about it, the people you keep closest to you will have the most influence on you.

God wants you to surround yourself with a crowd that has similar goals and dreams of success as you. Instead of them doubting and pulling you down, they will help build and encourage you. Make a decision today to surround yourself with like-minded friends that will help reach your goals.

Prayer for Today:

Father, thank You for caring about me. Remove people from my life that don't belong and add to my life friends that will help make me better. In Jesus' Name, Amen.

26
Stay Focused. Pay Attention.

Set your mind and keep focused habitually on the things above [the heavenly things], not on things that are on the earth [which have only temporal value]. Colossians 3:2, AMP

When your focus is divided, it makes it extremely difficult to give your all to one thing. In sports, the best way to develop in an area is to give that one area your undivided attention.

For example, professional athletes very rarely do full body workouts every day in the weight room. You will find that they have worked on a specific body part on a specific day. One day it may be biceps, triceps, and shoulders, and another day it may be hamstrings, quadriceps, and calves.

Focusing workouts on separate body parts on different days allows the athlete to focus more intently on that muscle group, which enhances the growth process of the athlete's muscles.

Likewise, your spiritual muscle building should be the same way. Your approach to reading the Bible should not involve shoving as much as you can into your head at one time. Break your Bible reading into sections, slow down and focus on what you have read.

If you only get through one paragraph that day, meditate on that truth until it becomes part of your life. Remember, when it comes to success, more does not always mean better. Only quality repetitions cause you to grow to your full potential.

Prayer for Today:

Father, thank You for helping me to focus on what will help me grow. Help me not to focus on things that will hurt me, but to focus on what Your Word says about me. In Jesus' Name, Amen.

27

We Love God Because He First Loved Us

I have loved you with an everlasting love, therefore with loving-kindness I have drawn you and continued my faithfulness to you. Jeremiah 31:3, AMP

We athletes can easily begin to focus on winning awards in return for stellar performances, which if we are not careful, can overtake our love for the game.

Understanding how much God loves you, releases you from the thought that you have missed out on what people have to offer you. Child of God, God's love is a gift.

All you have to do is receive it. It is an unconditional love that loves even in your worst moments. When you understand how valuable you are to God, it changes your desire to chase after Him rather than after things.

You would be surprised how much less you will care about popularity and acceptance once you grasp the reality of how God already accepts you. Understanding the Love of God will change your motive for why you play sports.

Trying to please people will no longer be your motive. God has always loved you. Remind yourself today of how valuable you are to God and watch how your confidence rises to new levels.

Prayer for Today:

Father, thank You for Your unconditional love that approves of me regardless of my mistakes. Thank You for accepting me for who I am, rather than what I do. I receive Your unfailing love. In Jesus' Name, Amen.

28
Meditation

This book of the law shall not depart out of your mouth, but you shall meditate on it day and night so that you may be careful to do everything written in it. Then you will be prosperous and successful. Joshua 1:8, NIV

Have you ever worried about possibly having a negative result happen in your game? Well, the good news is that if you know how to worry, then you know how to meditate. To meditate simply means to think about constantly, to ponder, to rehearse in one's mind over and over.

We all meditate every day, but the difference between having success or failure in any area is whether you are meditating on the right things. Joshua 1:8 makes it clear that meditating on God's Word brings prosperity and success.

For example, when you battle with fear you can go to the Bible and read 2 Timothy 1:7, *"God has not given you a spirit of fear, but of power, love, and a sound mind."* The more you read and meditate on this Scripture, the more God's boldness will rise inside you to kick out whatever fear you may have.

God not only wants you to be successful in sports but in your mind as well. A successful mindset will produce a successful performance. Don't allow your mind just to run all over the place, control your mind by taking a few minutes at the beginning of each day or before each game and meditate on God's Word.

You will never go wrong trusting in God's way to success.

Prayer for Today:

Father, thank You for helping me to train my mind to think more like you. Thank You for helping me learn Your Word so that I can play with confidence. In Jesus' Name, Amen.

29
Visualization, The Next Step To Goal Achievement

Write the vision and make it plain on tablets so he may run who reads it. Habakkuk 2:2, KJ2000

If someone sat you down in a room and wanted you to give a presentation on what you plan to accomplish this year with sports, and the strategy that you intend on using to accomplish your goal, would you be able to show a physical presentation that others could see with their own eyes?

Many athletes want to be successful, but they keep all of their goals and dreams stuck in their head. Dreams and ideas in your head are great, but you must get them out on paper so you and others can physically see and follow the plans to obtain your goals.

To fail to put your goals and strategies on paper is like weight lifting without a workout regime. It's easy to get off track. When your goals and ideas are on paper, it now becomes your blueprint for success.

Before any architect builds anything, he takes the ideas and designs that are in his head, and he draws what he wants the building to look like in great detail on a big sheet of paper. He constantly looks at the blueprints to continue to build the right structure. Likewise, when your goals and strategies are on paper, it allows you to move forward with the necessary adjustments.

Without your personal blueprint, it is easy to lose motivation or get tangled up in someone else's dream or goals. God wants you to bring life to your goals and dreams. Put them out in the open for you and others to see.

Prayer for Today:

Father, thank You for helping me stay motivated and helping me bring my dreams and goals to life. Thank You for helping me come up with a successful plan and strategy to accomplish the vision that You have for my life. In Jesus' Name, Amen.

30
Sticks And Stones May Break Your Bones And Words WILL Hurt You

The tongue can bring death or life; those who love to talk will reap the consequences. Proverbs 18:21, NLT

Did you know that your words have the power to affect you or someone else's life? Think about it, has anyone ever made a negative comment about you and you immediately got angry? What about when someone gave you a compliment, and you felt embarrassed? Both good and bad words spoken to you have the power to provoke different reactions or responses. Not only can someone else cause a different reaction in your attitude, but you have the power to change your emotions or attitude based on what you say to yourself. Many athletes continuously make negative statements about themselves and wonder why they keep getting negative results.

Well, I have great news for you. You can intentionally put yourself in a good mood by purposely speaking God's Word aloud over your life or situation. You believe more in what you say about yourself than what anyone else says. You are the prophet of your life. Every time you speak you sow seeds in your heart that will produce life or death. Commit today to speak words that establish your victory instead of your defeat.

Prayer for Today:

Father, thank You for giving me the power of life. Today, put a watch over my mouth to keep me from saying anything that will hurt me or my future. Help me to speak only on what will be beneficial to me and others around me. In Jesus' Name, Amen.

Prayer for Salvation

Just because you read this book does not mean that you are a Christian. Many people live every day with the belief that they are a Christian and on their way to Heaven because of their good behavior.

I am here to tell you that there is only one real way to experience this great life that God wants you to have. The real evidence of being a Christian is having Christ living on the inside of you. Christ comes to live on the inside of you when you confess with your mouth and believe in your heart that Jesus is your Lord and Savior.

In John 10:10 Jesus says, *"The thief's purpose is to kill, steal, and destroy, but my purpose is to give you a rich and satisfying life."* When you believe that Christ is your Savior, He sends the Holy Spirit to come live in you to help you live a victorious life. If you are unsure that you have truly received Christ as your Lord and Savior, confirm your salvation now by saying and believing this prayer:

Lord, I know that I need You in my life. I believe You died for my sins and rose from the dead. I trust and follow You as my Lord and Savior. Come into my heart and guide my life and help me to do Your will. In Your Name, Amen.

15 Positive Affirmations For Athletes

1. *I am a New Creature predestined for greatness.* **2 Corinthians 5:17**

2. *I am a Child of God fully accepted by the Father.* **John 1:12**

3. *I am loved by God regardless of how I perform.* **Romans 5:8**

4. *I am forgiven and will not be tormented by my past errors.* **1 John 1:9**

5. *I am an overcomer, and my faith is changing my circumstances.* **1 John 5:4**

6. *I am a giver, and God is causing people to help me prosper.* **2 Corinthians 9:8**

7. *I have authority over the devil, and no demon power can hurt me.* **Luke 10:17**

8. *Abundance is God's will for me, and I will not settle for less.* **John 10:10**

9. *I am healed, and sickness will not lord over my body.* **1 Peter 2:24**

10. *God is on my side; I will not fear.* **Psalm 118:6**

11. *The Holy Spirit is my helper, and I am never alone, and I have the peace of God.* **Philippians 4:7**

12. *I am blessed, and it's just a matter of time before things change what I see now is only temporary.* **Ephesians 1:3; 2 Corinthians 4:18**

13. *I have the wisdom of God; I hear the Father's voice; my steps are ordered by God and the voice of a stranger I will not follow.*

14. *I am set in the Body of Christ, and I know that I am valuable and important to the work of God.*
1 Corinthians 12:20-25; Ephesians 4:11-12

15. *I choose not to be offended, and I am being delivered out of all afflictions and persecutions.*

Matthew 5:10-12

The Author

Daryl Jones is available to speak for your club, church, team, banquet, retreat, and etc.
To inquire concerning your event, please email:
dJones@DestinySportsMission.com

www.ingramcontent.com/pod-product-compliance
Lightning Source LLC
Chambersburg PA
CBHW072105290426
44110CB00014B/1834